Peter Puzzlemaker

Returns!

Compiled and introduced by Martin Gardner

Dale Seymour
Publications

Project Editor: Mali Apple
Cover Design: David Woods
Art Director: Rachel Gage
Production: Terry Guyer

This book is published by Dale Seymour Publications, an imprint of the Alternative Publishing Group of Addison-Wesley Publishing Company.

Original design by George Carlson.

Originally published © 1922 by John Martin's House, Inc.
Order number DS21233
ISBN 0-86651-751-0

2 3 4 5 6 7 8 9 10 - MA - 97 96 95 94

DALE SEYMOUR PUBLICATIONS
P.O. BOX 10888
PALO ALTO, CA 94303

This book is printed on recycled paper.

Contents

Introduction by Martin Gardner v

The Puzzles 1

The Answers 89

George Carlson (1887–1962), a Connecticut graphic artist and cartoonist, was a major contributor to a monthly children's magazine called *John Martin's Book (JMB).* Throughout its two decades of existence—from 1913 to February 1933—Carlson illustrated dozens of its covers and drew hundreds of inside features.

JMB was edited by Carlson's friend, a whimsical New Yorker named Morgan Shepard. Shepard adopted the pseudonym John Martin in tribute to his mother who, when Shepard was a child, told him fanciful stories about the purple martins that nested each year in their yard. I will say no more about him or his periodical here because it would duplicate my introduction to the companion Peter Puzzlemaker book.

Carlson's most popular feature in *JMB* was a page on which a short, bespectacled Peter, dressed in the garb of a Pilgrim, presented a simple, entertaining word or mathematical problem. To the delight of child readers, each picture included an amusing mistake. Answers to both puzzles and mistakes were wisely held over for the following issue.

In 1922 John Martin's House published a hardcover collection of Peter Puzzlemaker pages from the earliest issue of *JMB* in October 1918 through the issue for the end of November 1922. Seventy years later, in 1992, a new edition of the book was printed by Dale Seymour Publications. This sequel, *Peter Puzzlemaker Returns!,* which I had the pleasure of assembling, takes up where the previous book left off, catching Peter Puzzlemaker pages from January 1923 through December 1925.

The first Peter Puzzlemaker book included puzzles and riddles that Carlson illustrated specifically for the book. In *Peter Puzzlemaker Returns!* I have reprinted riddles he illustrated for the magazine prior to 1925, as well as pictures that magically turn into something different when rotated 180 degrees. Carlson was not the first to create upside-down art, though he was the first to contribute such pictures frequently to a children's magazine.

During a later period he drew scenes crammed with objects whose names began with a certain letter. Each letter of the alphabet was represented in the series. I have included only the first four, pictures for the letters A, B, C, and D.

Many of the riddle pictures appearing here are signed "Gookel." I have no idea why Carlson used this bizarre pseudonym. We know that the art is his because his style is clearly recognizable, and because in many cases he was identified as the artist in the magazine's contents.

In keeping with the content of *JMB,* Carlson kept his puzzles on a level suitable for children of ages seven to eleven. Only rarely did he slip in a problem that would be difficult even for parents; the mutilated checkerboard is a good example.

In my opinion Carlson had no equal as a puzzle maker for the very young. Little has been written about Carlson. Apart from my essay "John Martin's Book: An Almost Forgotten Children's Magazine" (*Children's Literature,* Vol. 18, 1990), and aside from a few newspaper interviews, the only tributes to Carlson have been in histories of comic books. The most recent at this writing is a short piece in *The Smithsonian Book of Comic Book Comics* by Michael Barrier and Martin Williams (Abrams, 1982). It reprints in color twenty pages from Carlson's *Jingle-Jangle Comics.* Comic book collectors and historians generally know Carlson only for this work and a few rare issues of a comic book devoted to puzzles. They have yet to discover his much more important and prolific contributions to *JMB.*

Martin Gardner

HERE'S a jumble, rough and tumble, mixy, trixy alphabet:
Can you match 'em? Can you catch 'em?
See how many you can get.
A—B—C—D—please go E Z: Twenty-six letters stout.
Scratch and scramble monogram—
Can YOU pick the letters out?

PETER Puzzlemaker is here to wish you a Happy New Year, and he shows you, by changing one letter at a time, how to make *old* into *new*. The New Year's thought is a good motto to remember, once you have made it out. There is a mistake in the picture, too.

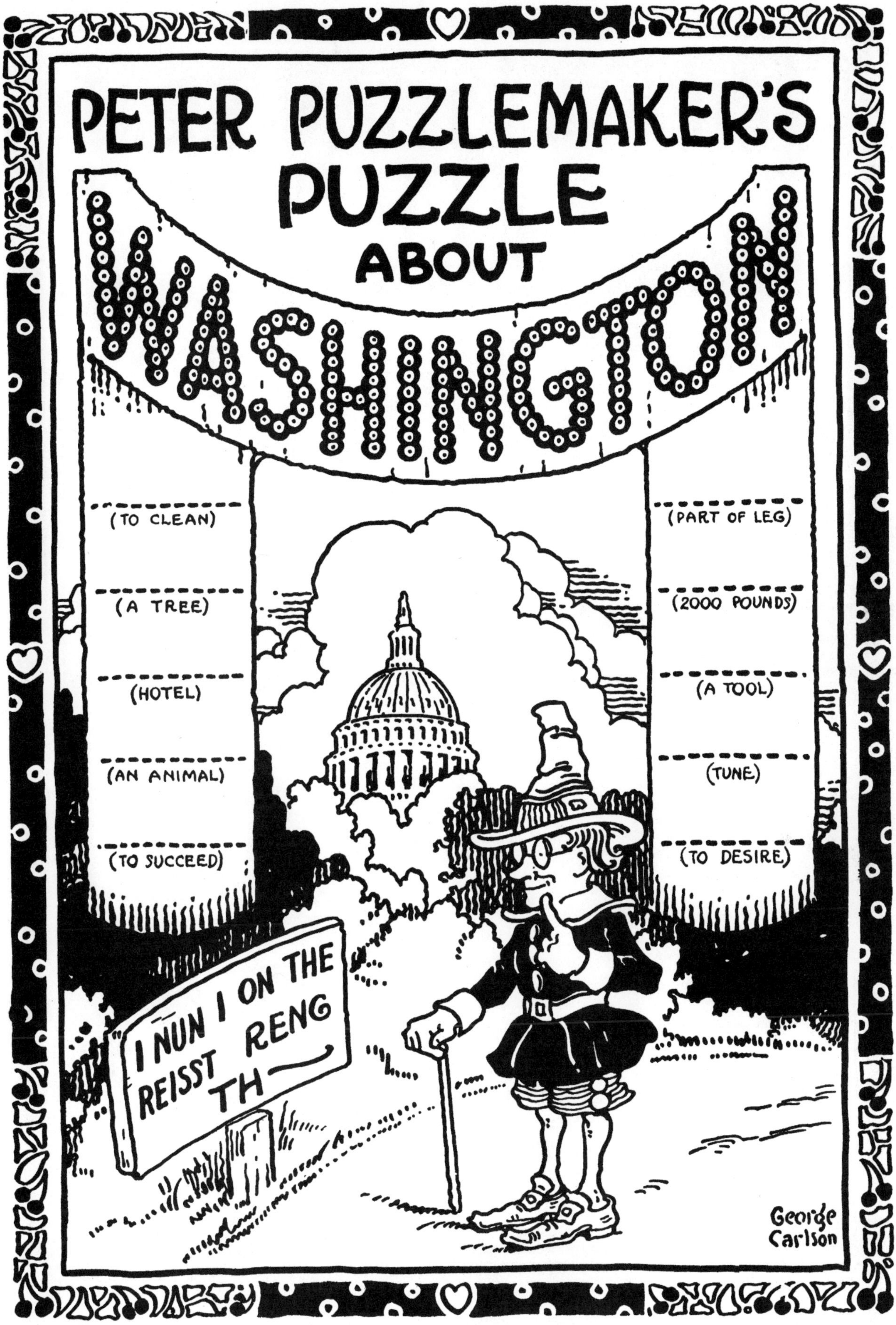

WHEN Peter Puzzlemaker sees the word *Washington* he also sees many other words concealed in it. By using only the letters in this word he has found ten other words. The meaning of each is indicated below the dotted line. Write the words on the lines, and then see how many more you can find. There is a fitting motto on the sign, and something is wrong in the picture.

VALENTINE'S DAY finds Peter Puzzlemaker sending this valentine. The word *Valentine* has many other words hidden in it. See if you can write a word for each meaning written under the dotted lines, and also see how many more you can find, using only the letters found in *Valentine*. Johnny Elf has a good motto for you in that jumble of letters, and there is something missing in the picture.

EVEN at the table, Peter likes to puzzle his brain, and perhaps sometimes he isn't quite sure what he is going to get. Can you read the six items on his lunch menu? Read the motto below, and find something wrong in the picture.

UP-SIDE-DOWN-SIDE-UP

HERE'S A FUNNY KIND OF BIRD
YOU NEVER SAW BEFORE ---

TURN HIS PICTURE UPSIDE DOWN
IT'S PUSS BEHIND THE DOOR

↑UP – DOWN↓

A Riddle

TELL what goes down the chimney *down*
(Oh, yes indeed it can, Sir.)
But won't go up the chimney *up*?
(Now try and give the answer.)

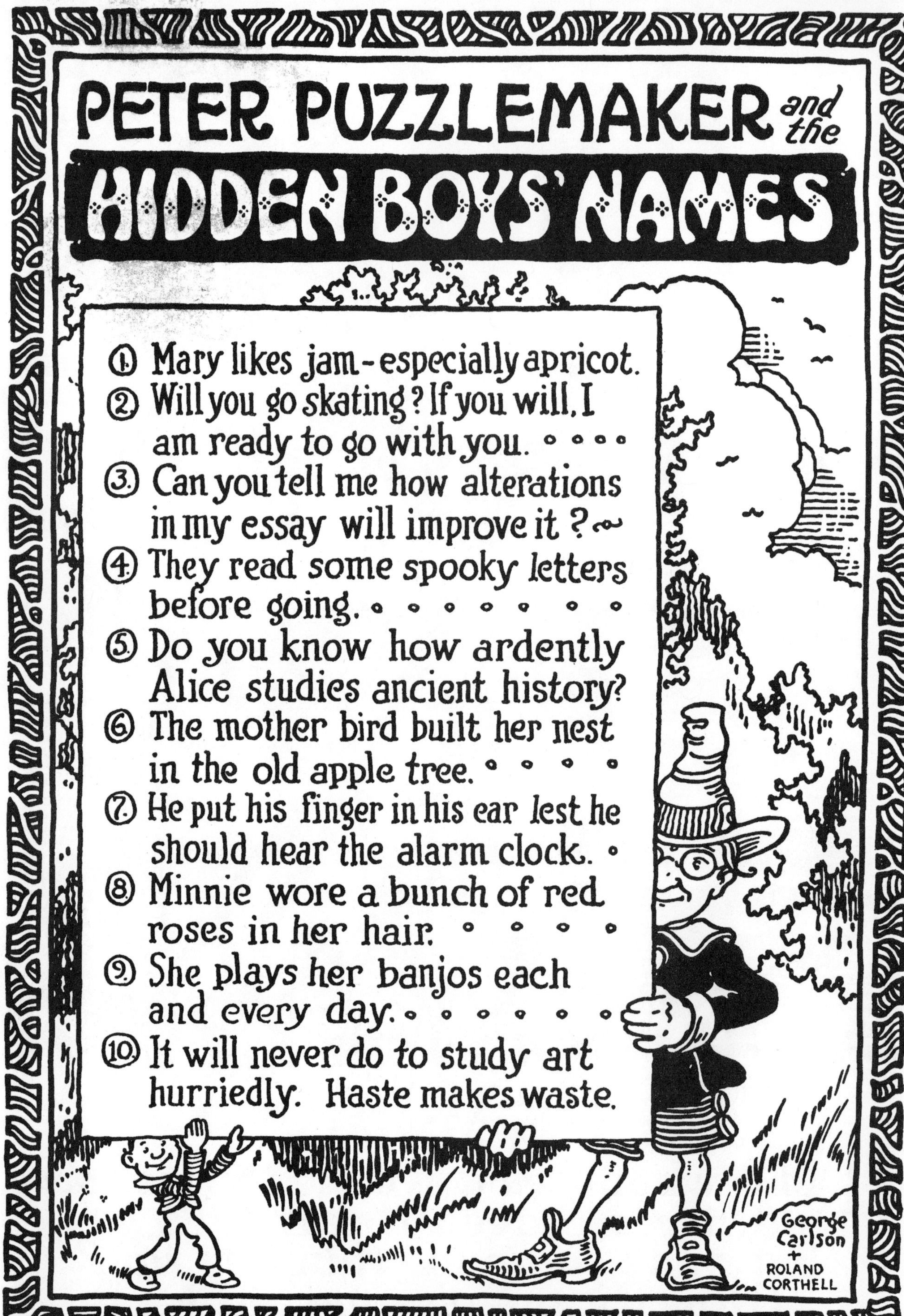

IN THE ten sentences Peter is holding before you, he has hidden the names of ten boys. He thinks you ought to find them in ten minutes. Can you? There is a funny little mistake in the picture, too.

PETER PUZZLEMAKER and The 3 MATCHES

CAN you help Peter make four out of his three matches without breaking them or splitting them in any way? Lynette Elf has another question about the same matches. See if you can solve these questions, unravel the motto on the sign, and find what is missing in the picture.

WHILE reading a book the other day, Peter Puzzlemaker came across three sentences with words that contained the same letters but in different positions. He has left blanks where the words should go, each word having four letters and a different set of letters for each sentence. As usual, there is something wrong in the picture. What is it?

IN the ten sentences Peter is showing you, he has hidden the names of ten girls. Can you find them? Jared Elf says that by changing two of the letters in the name he is holding, you will get the name of a country. What is missing in this picture?

UP-SIDE-DOWN-SIDE-UP

HERE'S A BUNNY IN HER HOUSE
EATING UP A CARROT ~ ~ ~

TURN THE PICTURE UPSIDE DOWN
AND FIND A FUNNY PARROT

KIT ~ T

A Riddle

WHEN is a little Kitten like
A *teapot* Full of tea?
The answer is as easy as
An easy ease can be.

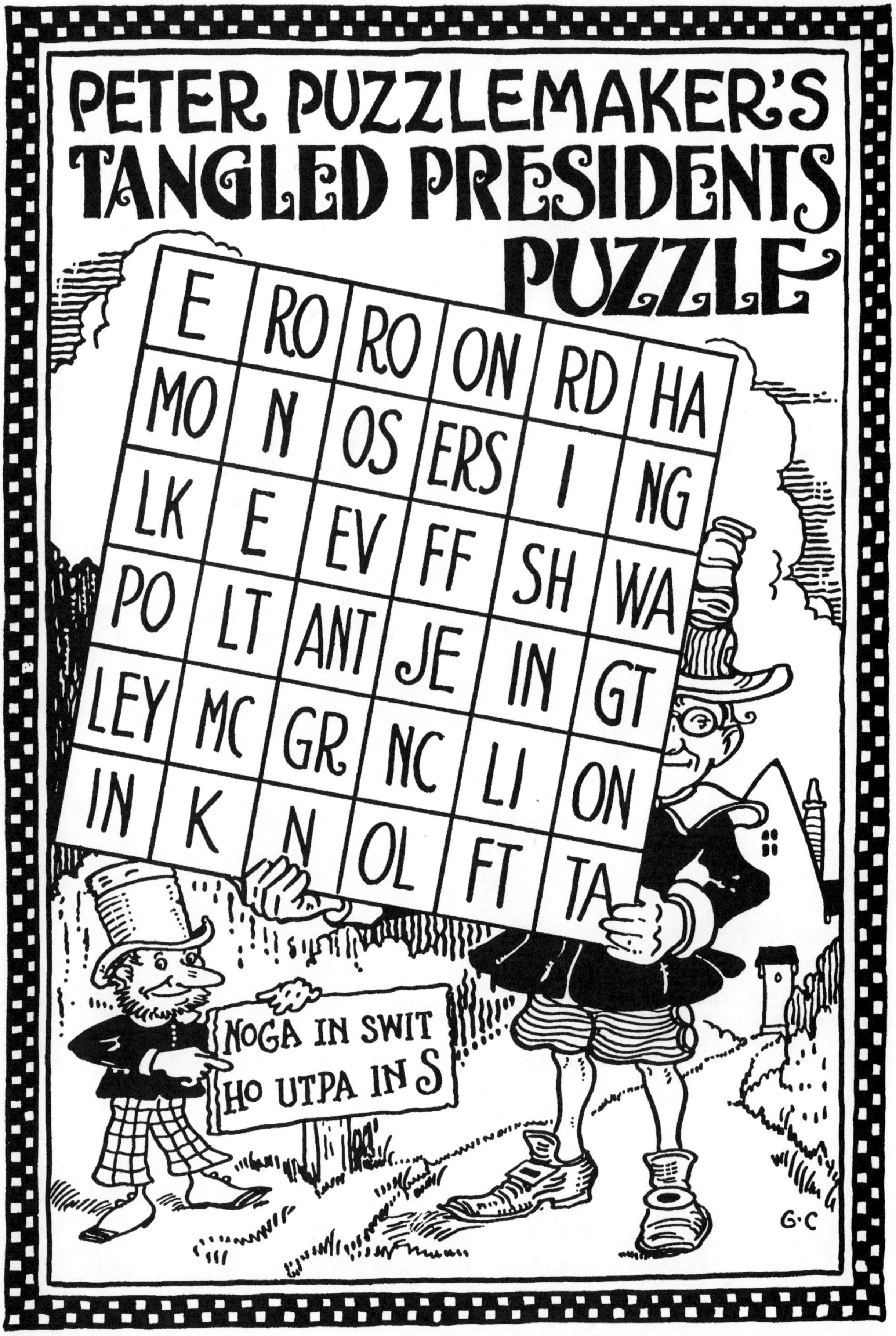

IN the squares Peter is holding you will find the names of ten Presidents of the United States. Can you start from one of the squares and draw a line through adjoining squares and read the ten names? See if you can read what the little man has painted on the sign and also find what is wrong in the picture.

IN THE sentences Peter has here before you, he has left out certain words. On each sign, the missing words all contain the same letters. Each sentence requires a different set of words. Can you fill them in? There is something missing in the picture, and Elsie Elf has a motto puzzle for you to solve.

SOME careless person has broken Peter's checkerboard and has set it together again all wrong. Can you cut it in only two pieces and join them together to make a perfect checkerboard? The strange monogram on the sign by Peter's feet represents the name of a country. Can you tell what it is, and also what is wrong with the picture?

PETER PUZZLEMAKER and the BALLOONS

HERE is a balloon seller showing Peter a puzzle with letters on the balloons. See how many boys' names you can find by starting from any letter and going to the next one in any direction. There is a mistake for you to find in the picture, and the balloon seller has her business motto on the basket printed wrong. How should it read?

3 PUZZLE NOTES

Help the Old Man of Dee to read the three notes.~ Fill the blanks with appropriate words all containing the same letters. Each note has a different set of letters.

WHERE ARE THEY?

CAN YOU FIND THE FARMER'S TWO COWS?

CAN YOU FIND THE TWO HORSES FOR THE HORSESHOER?

UP-SIDE-DOWN-SIDE-UP

HERE IN BRAND-NEW HAT AND TIE-
IS MISTER JAKE McPHLISTER.

TURN THE PICTURE ROUND ABOUT
AND SEE HIS CHARMING SISTER!

HOUSE AND HORSE
A Riddle

WHEN is a house just like a horse?
When it has blinds upon it.
When is a house like a rusty clock?
When it is hard to run it.

PETER PUZZLEMAKER and his POND

OUT on his farm Peter has a little square pond with a tree at each corner. He wants to double the size of this pond without moving the trees and still have the pond square. Can you help him? Huang has a sign to be put up by the pond, and if you change one letter in each word it will read correctly. There is something wrong in the picture, too.

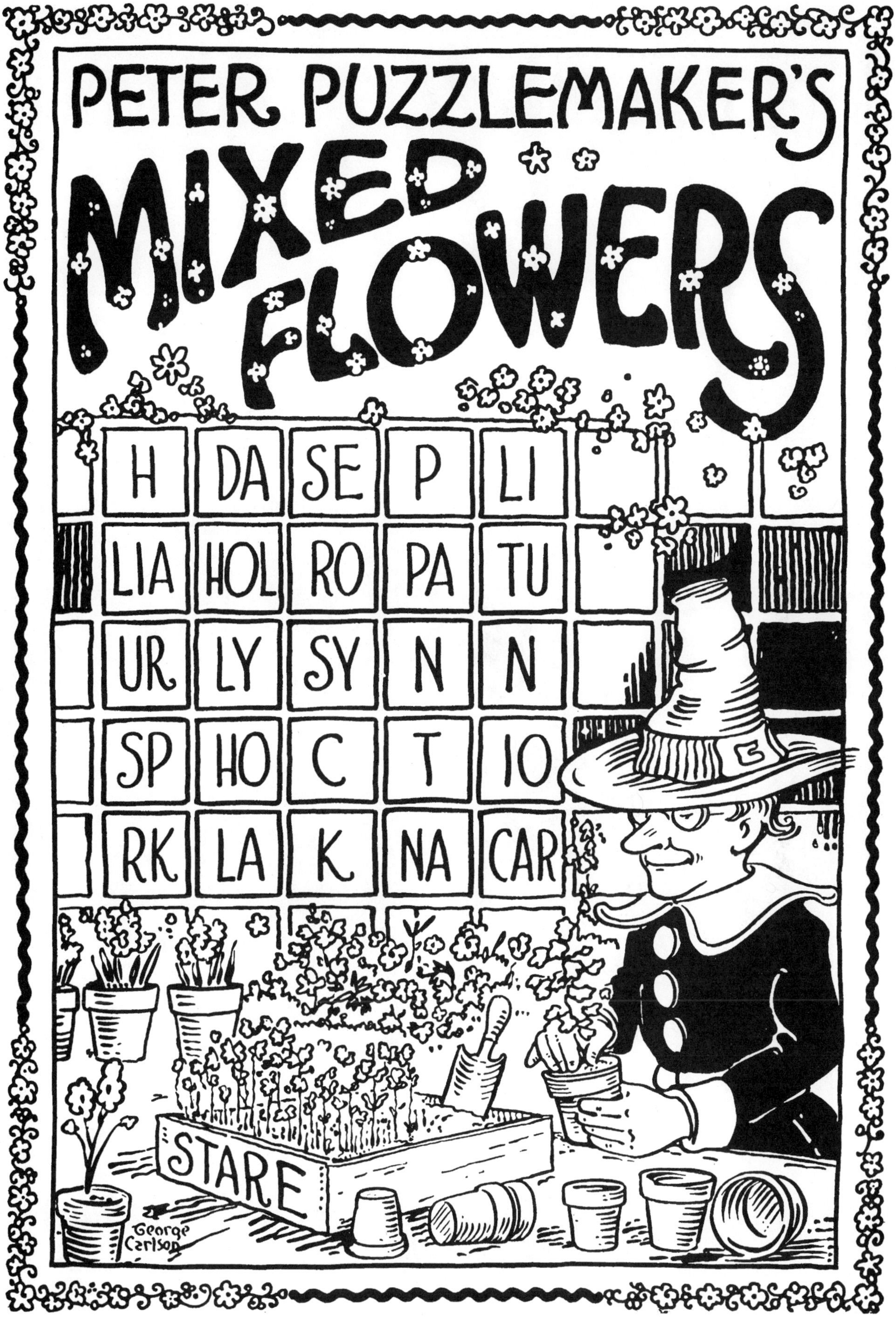

IN HIS greenhouse Peter has made a neat little puzzle on the window panes. Beginning in one of the squares and moving to an adjoining one, you can read the names of seven flowers. On the flower box there is the name of another flower. Can you rearrange the letters to spell it right? And what is missing in this picture?

PETER PUZZLEMAKER'S PUZZLE-SIGNS

HERE we see Peter meeting three people carrying signs with odd sentences painted on them. Certain words are left out that contain the same letters. Each sentence requires a different set of words. Can you fill them in? And what does the elf's sign say? There is also a mistake in this picture for you to find.

IN PETER'S puzzle store there is a canned-goods department. This has made Peter think of many words beginning with *C-A-N*, and he has made these labels with the meaning of fifteen words that begin with *CAN*. Can you tell what they are, what is wrong in this picture, and how much Ami is going to spend?

PETER PUZZLEMAKER'S
"A" PUZZLE
PRIVATE SCHOOL ANNEX
E.S. O'BRIEN
USE
NOTICE
PETS
LONG ALLEY
MAPS
HOW MANY THINGS CAN YOU FIND IN THIS PICTURE BEGINNING WITH LETTER "A"?
G.C.

B
B
PETER PUZZLEMAKER'S
"B" PUZZLE
MEAT MARKET
HAIRCUTS
BAKERY
VEGETABLES
EXPRESS
HOW MANY THINGS CAN YOU FIND IN THIS PICTURE BEGINNING WITH LETTER "B"?
B
B

UP-SIDE-DOWN-SIDE-UP

HERE'S A GENTLE MOOLY COW
BY AN UPRIGHT LOG

TURN THE PICTURE ROUND LIKE THIS
AND FIND A FUNNY FROG

SPEED
A Riddle

WHICH goes the faster, heat or cold?
Why heat, for don't you see
You can catch cold, but can't catch heat,
That's plain as plain can be.

PETER has arranged a jolly Christmas tree party for his friends, and the presents are all wrapped. You can tell what they are by spelling out letters in the chart, starting from certain letters and moving into the next square in any direction. There are ten presents and there is also something missing in the picture. Tito Elf has his Christmas card all mixed up. How should it read?

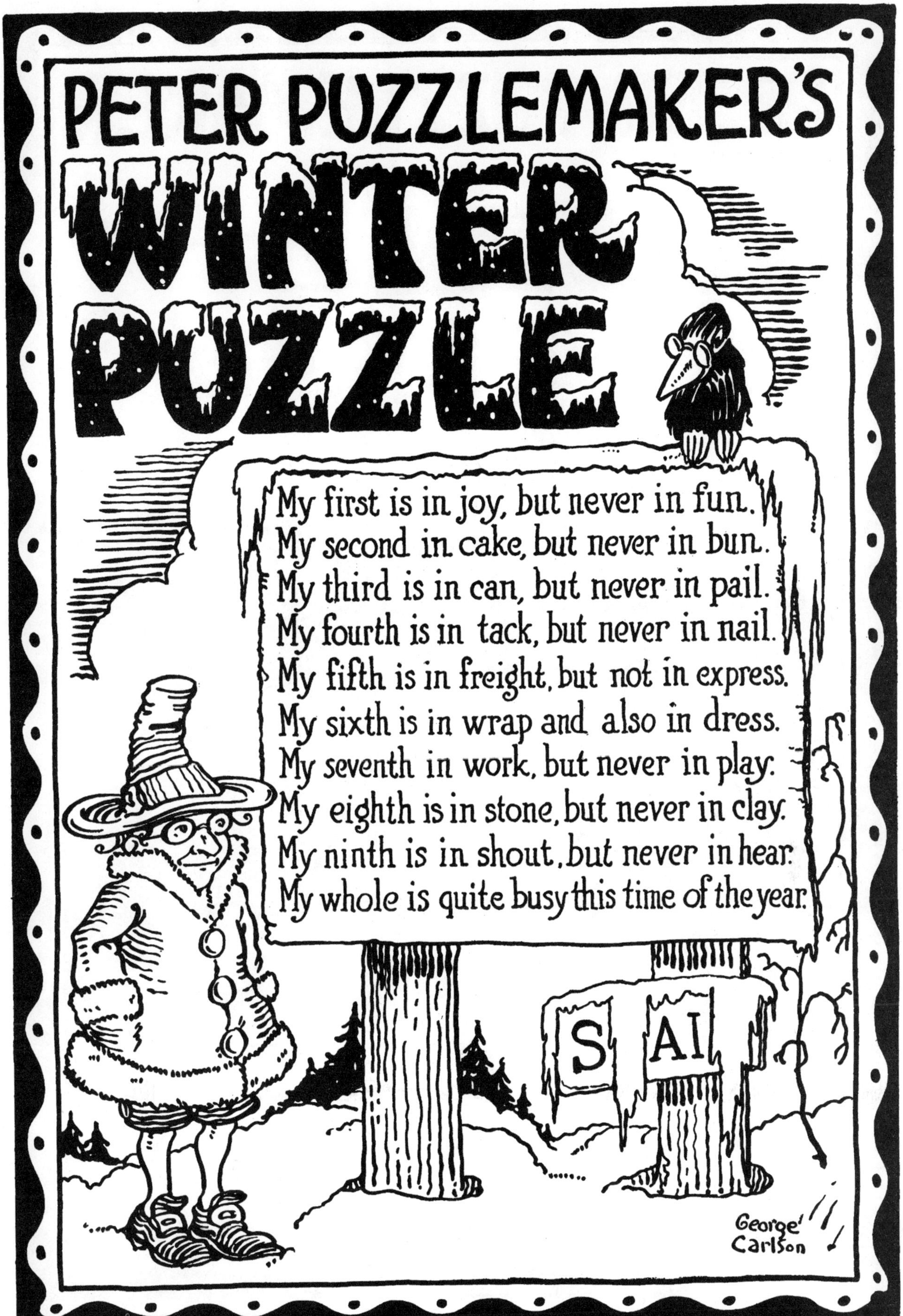

HERE is Peter's winter puzzle. Read the verse and find the letters that will make the name of a well-known winter character. On the small sign the icicles have hidden two letters in a word. Which two will make the name of a country, an animal, or part of a house? Also see if you can find what is wrong in this picture.

PETER has received a package from a friend. Before he can open it, he must solve the puzzle on the outside and find out what is in it. On each line write a word of four letters, the meaning of which is underneath. Begin each word with a capital. The capitals will spell what Peter is getting. There is something missing in the picture, and if you rearrange the letters on the flowerpot you will find the name of a plant.

DOWN the street near Peter's house is a jewelry shop. On the puzzle sign are the names of six precious stones. If you start from certain hexagons and move to the next one in any direction, you will spell them out. Ana is there with her little puzzle, too. She holds up the name of a valuable metal but the letters are a little mixed up. Then there is a mistake in the picture, too.

UP-SIDE-DOWN-SIDE-UP

SEE THE DUCKS UPON PARADE
LISTEN TO THEM QUACK!

TURN THE PICTURE AND YOU'LL SEE
A CLOWN UPON HIS BACK

A Timely Riddle

What runs, yet has no feet to walk,
And tells us much, but cannot talk;
That has two hands, a face quite round,
Can softly make a tiny sound??
Here in these lines its name is found.

PETER PUZZLEMAKER IN SPRINGTIME

SPRING in Puzzleland finds Peter looking over his flower garden for signs of the season. Here we see him looking at the shoots of his favorite spring flower. On the board he has a puzzle sum that tells the name of the flower. Add or subtract (as shown) the names of the objects and you will solve the sum. Also see if you can tell what is missing in the picture.

PETER PUZZLEMAKER'S CONCEALED PRESIDENTS

HERE we have a puzzle about Presidents. The names of five of them are hidden in the sentences, and Peter is telling Joshua Crow who they are. In his beak Joshua has the name of one of our more recent Presidents, but he has not put down the letters quite right. Can you fix them, and also find something in the picture that is not as it should be?

A LITTLE girl in a great big state sent this puzzle to Peter. Pick out the right letters in the fruits and you will spell out the girl's state. Hilary Elf is thinking of fruit, too. Fix her letters the right way and you will see what it is. Can you see anything wrong in the picture?

WHILE visiting the zoo the other day, Peter saw seven strange sentences painted on the wall. Each sentence had the name of an animal hidden in it. Can you find them as easily as Peter did? Edgar Elf holds up a card to you and says it is the name of an animal. Can you tell what that is, as well as what is missing in the picture?

UP-SIDE-DOWN-SIDE-UP

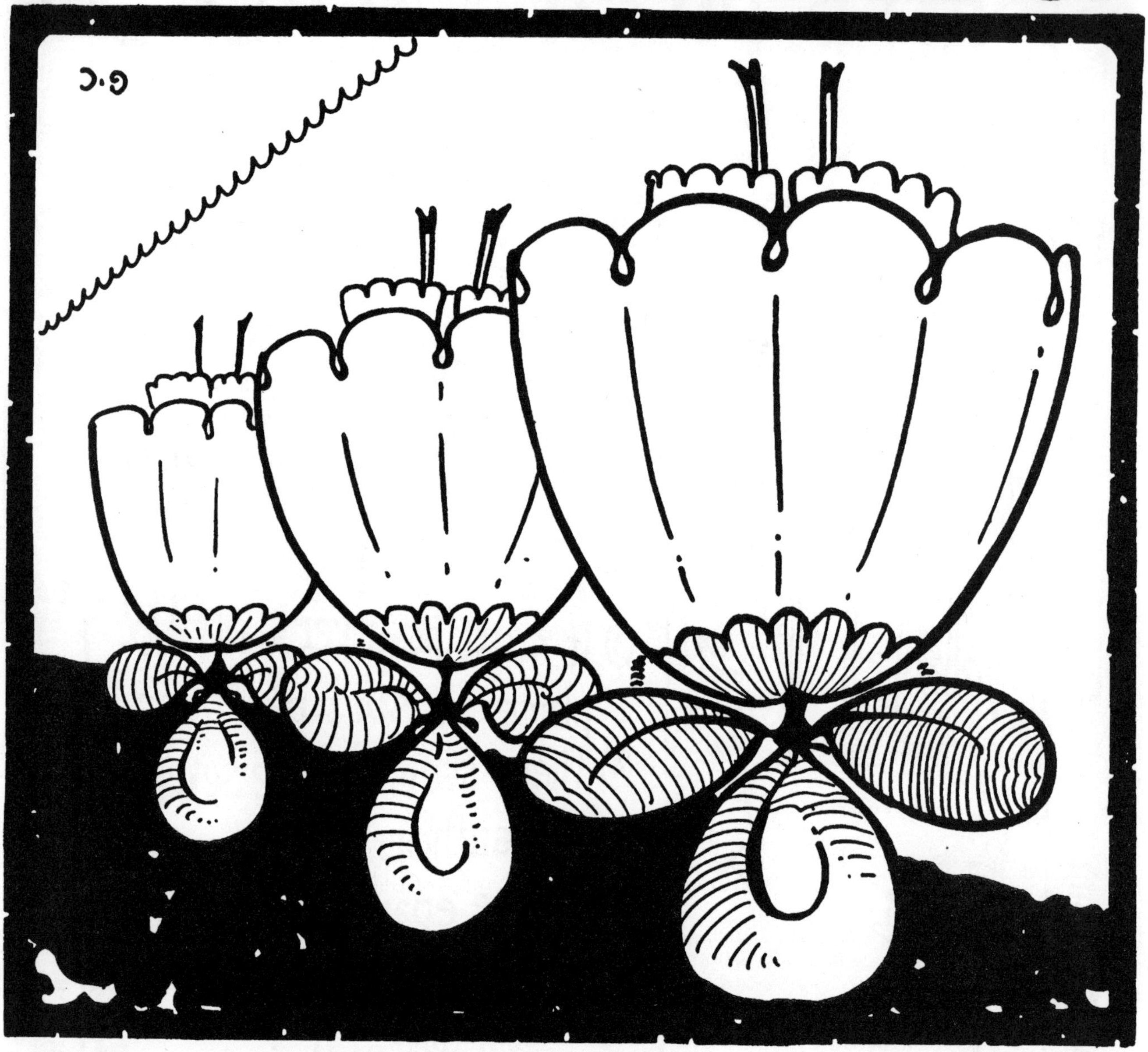

WHAT ARE THESE FLOWERS LARGE & STRANGE
THAT IN A ROW I SEE?

WE'LL TURN THE PICTURE ROUND ABOUT
AND FIND THE SISTERS THREE.

WEIGHT

A Riddle

OF Mr. Fish, what part weighs most?
(This riddle may seem easy.)
The answer is an easy one.
The scales weigh most, you see.

PETER PUZZLEMAKER and the TWO ANIMALS

PETER is telling his little dog about two of his other animal companions. Solve the puzzle and you will know what they are. In the spaces of each line, write a word, the meaning of which is given at the side. The first and last letters, reading down, will spell the names of the animals. The letters on the dog's collar, rearranged, will spell his name. What is missing in the picture?

PETER Puzzlemaker has made up seven sentences. In each one, the name of an animal is hidden away. Jack Elf found them in seven minutes exactly. He also has a puzzle sentence for you to work out. Something in the picture is not quite finished. What is it?

PETER Puzzlemaker is studying. The letters in the title of his book are a little out of order, but if you will rearrange them you will see what kind of book it is. In the sentences above are hidden the names of five Presidents. Help Peter find them, and tell what is wrong in the picture.

PETER PUZZLEMAKER'S DINNER PUZZLE

O	C	K	L	B	S
F	S	E	R	U	O
F	E	Y	E	T	P
I	S	O	T	A	D
R	E	N	M	E	I
R	B	A	R	C	P

HERE is Peter's Thanksgiving dinner. He is just asking his guest what she likes. The answer, which is oddly spelled, also tells, when the letters are rearranged, what she will say after dinner. The letters in the squares spell at least twelve things that Peter will eat. Spell them out by moving from one square to the next in any direction. What is missing in this picture?

UP-SIDE-DOWN-SIDE-UP

POOR KITTY'S RATHER WORRIED
WHAT IS IT MAKES HER SO?

JUST TURN THE PICTURE UPSIDE DOWN
AND THEN YOU'LL SURELY KNOW!

A RIDDLE

IF YOU judge by our whiteness and hardness alone,
You might take us for fragments of crystalline stone;
But plunge us in water, and what will ensue?
We shall pass out of sight—a thing stone would not do.
Yet, though we completely escape from your eyes,
By means of your taste you may still recognize
Our presence; for when we have vanished from view,
You will find we have sweetened the water for you.

What are we?

PETER PUZZLEMAKER'S REVIEW

SHOWING SOME of the MANY GOOD PUZZLES SENT IN BY HIS LITTLE FRIENDS

WHERE SHALL THE MAIL CARRIER TAKE THIS LETTER?

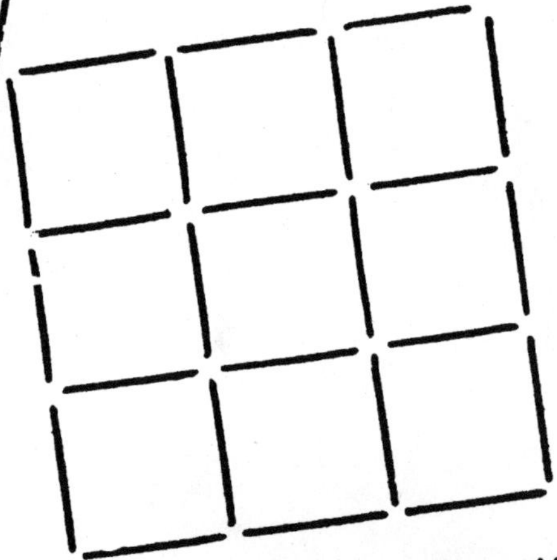

LAY OUT 24 TOOTHPICKS LIKE THIS REMOVE 8 AND LEAVE 2 SQUARES

A PUZZLE NOTE Can you read it?

Doctor X Dr. to X the th) Standing Miss (em

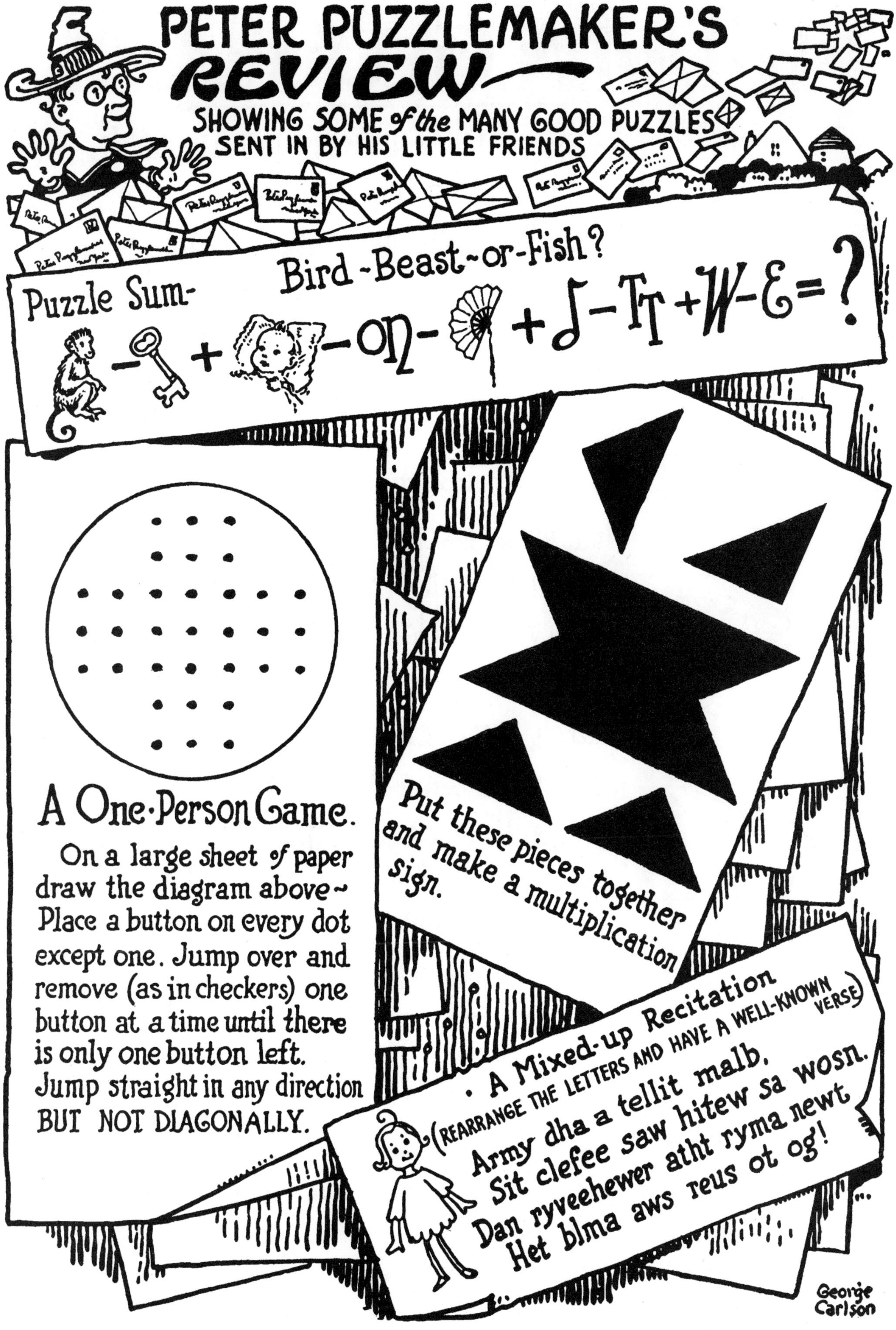
PETER PUZZLEMAKER'S
REVIEW
SHOWING SOME of the MANY GOOD PUZZLES
SENT IN BY HIS LITTLE FRIENDS
Puzzle Sum-
Bird-Beast-or-Fish?
- + -on- + - TT + W - E = ?
A One-Person Game.
On a large sheet of paper draw the diagram above~ Place a button on every dot except one. Jump over and remove (as in checkers) one button at a time until there is only one button left. Jump straight in any direction BUT NOT DIAGONALLY.
Put these pieces together and make a multiplication sign.
· A Mixed-up Recitation
(REARRANGE THE LETTERS AND HAVE A WELL-KNOWN VERSE)
Army dha a tellit malb,
Sit clefee saw hitew sa wosn.
Dan ryveehewer atht ryma newt
Het blma aws reus ot og!
George Carlson

HIDDEN GEOGRAPHY?

Ala.
Alaska
Ariz.
Ark.
Calif.
Colo.
Conn.
Del.
Fla.
Ga.
Hawaii
Idaho
Ill.
Ind.
Iowa
Kans.
Ky.
La.
Maine
Md.
Mass.
Mich.
Minn.
Miss.
Mo.
Mont.
Nebr.
Nev.
N.H.
N.J.
N.Mex.
N.Y.
N.C.
N.Dak.
Ohio
Okla.
Oreg.
Pa.
R.I.
S.C.
S.Dak.
Tenn.
Tex.
Utah
Vt.
Va.
Wash.
W.Va.
Wis.
Wyo.

1 The group was made up mainly of laughing girls and boys.

2. I am denied many things I want but don't need.

3. In a dense fog a good pair of ears is better than good eyes.

4. We must not forget that all about us are those who need help.

5. What excuse has one for not doing his duty?

6 The gum issuing from some trees is very valuable.

7. I had good luck yesterday in my search for orchids.

8. Nine out of ten newspapers told of the startling occurrences.

9. I saw him on the first day of the month.

10. How shallow is the reasoning of those who judge others by themselves.

An abbreviation of the name of a state is hidden in each one of the ten sentences. A list of the state abbreviations is at the side to help you find the hidden states.

WHO IS THE BIGGEST?

BUNNY, Puppy, Mr. Bruin,
All upon an airing bent,
Are an optical illusion
Causing heated argument.

Not which one is very stylish,
Nor the one whose ears are longest;
Neither has a word been spoken
Of the one who is the strongest.

Maybe *you* can settle matters;
Say which one is really smallest,
And without a rule or compass
Tell me which one is the *tallest*.

MISS·MONAD

THIS PERSON HAS A DOUBLE-FACE;
MISS MONAD IS HER NAME
FOR UPSIDE DOWN OR DOWN-SIDE UP
SHE ALWAYS LOOKS THE SAME,

I THRIVE in the vegetable garden,
In rain and in sunshine, along
With carrot and spinach and radish,
But they grow not nearly so strong!

Now listen, I'll tell you a secret—
I know it will be a surprise—
When cook dresses me for the table,
She always has tears in her eyes.

What am I?

ONE evening Peter heard a fine radio program from ________—well, he'll let you figure out the names of the two cities. He has made them into puzzle pictures. Write down the words the pictures represent. All the words have four letters, except one that has three letters and one that is an abbreviation for a musical instrument. The first and last letters will spell out the two cities. Can you see what is wrong in this picture?

PETER PUZZLEMAKER'S CHAT

A REBUS

The rebus, or picture puzzle, is an old-time favorite. Here we have one that represents a former President.

WORD JUMPING

By changing one letter in the word at a time, turn BLUE into PINK in ten moves.

B L U E

_ _ _ _

_ _ _ _

_ _ _ _

_ _ _ _

_ _ _ _

_ _ _ _

_ _ _ _

_ _ _ _

_ _ _ _

P I N K

A RAINY DAY PUZZLE

A careful grocer wrapping up a bottle of olive oil for a girl is the subject of the title for this picture. By changing around the same letters, can you make another suitable title?

The RIDDLE CORNER

What is it that the living and the dead do at the same time?

Why is six afraid of seven?

What is smaller than a flea's mouth?

When will water stop running downhill?

When a girl falls in the water, what is the first thing she does?

PETER'S black cat, Snowball, and his white dog, Sooty, have a little problem for you. Can you change a black cat into a white dog? Change one letter in each word at a time and in eight moves, and you will have it. Under each of the lines is a hint of the word that is supposed to be there. Can you find the strange thing that was left out of the picture?

IS IT A VALENTINE?

Here is an anagram for you! I rather suspect that someone has left it for me as a valentine. Well, then, twist the letters into their right places and see what the name of our muffled friend is and also *his* good friend.

A FLOWER CHARADE

Here is a puzzle called a charade. Can you puzzle out what the secret word is?

My first is in rose, not in geranium.
My second in geranium, but not in pansy.
My third is in pansy, but not in foxglove.
My fourth is in foxglove, but not in lily.
My fifth is in lily and also in goldenrod.
My sixth is in goldenrod, but not in wisteria.
My seventh is in wisteria, but not everlasting.
My eighth is in everlasting and also in real.
My ninth is in real and also in forget-me-not.
My whole is the name of a very large flower.

WORD JUMPING

By changing one letter in the word at a time, change OWL into BAT in six moves.

O W L
— — —
— — —
— — —
— — —
— — —
B A T

A REBUS

Here's a rebus that will have you guessing! What foreign country does this picture represent?

A KITCHEN CHARADE

My first is in stove, but never in cook.
My second in meat is never in hook.
My third is in lamb, but never in pork.
My fourth is in teaspoon, but never in fork.
My whole with our food is good for its flavor,
And its use in the kitchen is something to savor.

UP-SIDE-DOWN-SIDE-UP

HOW WOULD YOU LIKE A CUP OF TEA
FROM SUCH A FANCY POT?

WHEN UPSIDE DOWN THE PICTURE SHOWS
THE ANCIENT KING of SWAT!

THERE'S a funny, brown fellow down under the ground;
Though his house is quite dark, he can look all around.
"And how can he see?" a little girl cries.
Why, this funny, brown fellow is covered with eyes!

What is it?

PETER has been star-gazing! And here is his new puzzle for you. The top star in the picture is really a planet. Its name of five letters, when placed in the correct blank spaces on the points, should help you make words reading into the center and all ending with the same letter. The other star is a well-known constellation. Do the same thing with this one. What is wrong in the picture?

PETER PUZZLEMAKER'S CHAT

PRESIDENTIAL WORD SQUARE

Fill the blank spaces with the name of a well-known President so that the other letters will make a true word, reading both horizontally and vertically.

DOUBLE ACROSTIC

Place the eight four-letter words defined below one underneath the other. The first letters will spell out the name of an American poet, and the last ones the name of an English poet.

Desire. — — — —

House. — — — —

A metal. — — — —

A small city. — — — —

A flat dish for serving. — — — —

Pupil of the eye. — — — —

Reflected sound. — — — —

Water from the clouds. — — — —

HIDDEN COUNTRIES

The names of five countries are concealed in the following sentences. Can you find them?

In such a wind I am almost powerless.

She had new zeal and zest for the story.

Can a daily paper be printed every month?

Can an ape run thirty miles?

We had broken yams for dinner.

We wouldn't miss this; we'd enter.

A MUSICAL CHARADE

Can you solve this charade?
My first is in heavy, but never in light.
My second in music is also in might.
My third is in note, but never in clef,
My fourth is in louder, but never in deaf,
My fifth in sing is never in sound,
My sixth in band is also in pound,
My whole with deep melody having its place
In making fine music and taking up space.

The RIDDLE CORNER

What is it that a cat has, but no other animal?
What contains more feet in winter than in summer?
When is a horse like a house?

PEOPLE have planted 16 trees in the park, all equal distances apart. They have offered a reward if a path can be laid out that would surround each tree and make a symmetrical design. Can you find it? Starting at the X, draw a line around each dot without lifting your pencil. The path must return to its starting point at X, and it must look exactly the same when the page is turned on its side and upside down. What is missing in this picture?

PETER PUZZLEMAKER'S CHAT

GIRL'S NAME WORD SQUARE

Fill the blank spaces with the name of a girl so that the other letters will make words, reading both horizontally and vertically.

A REBUS

Here's a rebus that will have you guessing! What country does this represent?

WORD JUMPING

By changing one letter in the word at a time, make DOOR into LOCK in four moves.

D O O R

_ _ _ _

_ _ _ _

_ _ _ _

L O C K

A PUZZLE SUM

Add and subtract the things in this picture and the answer will be the name of a well-known animal.

HIDDEN CITIES

The names of five European cities are concealed in the following sentences:

He took a flying leap, a risky thing to do.

The spoils of the robber lined the inside of the gloomy cave.

There was a sleepy fat hen sitting on her nest.

There he was, like a nomad, riding about on the desert.

She will always trail on donkeys.

PETER PUZZLEMAKER'S
"C" PUZZLE
HOW MANY THINGS
CAN YOU FIND IN THIS PICTURE
BEGINNING WITH LETTER "C"?
GROCERIES
BISCUIT
BEST
COFFEE
BON
BONS
15¢
George
Carlson

PETER PUZZLEMAKER'S
"D" PUZZLE
PETER
DRAWN BY DORIS
DIPLOMA
Peter Puzzlemaker
Doctor in Puzzology
JUNE
12
LEXICON
DEED
DENTIST
DETOUR
M.D.
HOW MANY THINGS CAN YOU FIND IN THIS PICTURE BEGINNING WITH LETTER "D"?

MIX-UPS

OPEN · BURNS · COLOR · HOP · CROAK ·

· RUSTS · MELTS · MOO · TEARS · CUT ·

· GROW · SWIM · WORK · SCRATCH · BLOOM ·

· HOOT · PLAY · GRUNT · FLY · LEARN ·

THE WORDS UNDER THE PICTURES ARE IN THE WRONG PLACE. ~ SEE IF YOU CAN FIND THE RIGHT PICTURE FOR EACH ONE.

FOOD

A Riddle

WHY is it quite impossible
To starve for lack of food or fare
In the Sahara Desert, dears?
Because of the sand which is there.

I am going to give you a travel puzzle. It will be easy for you to tell where I'm going after you study the route map. If you start from certain circles and go to an adjoining one in any direction, you will spell out abbreviations of seven states I will visit. Also, when rightly arranged the letters on my suitcase will spell out the name of a city where I have done a lot of sightseeing. There is a mistake in the picture, too.

PETER PUZZLEMAKER'S CHAT

HIDDEN FLOWERS

The names of five flowers are concealed in the following sentences.

He soon returned, for he ran very fast errands.

Up in Canada I systematized the work for them.

While George ran, I umpired the game.

A score of zero seemed too low.

The great span symbolized the best in the art of building bridges.

A NECKTIE PUZZLE

This is a form of puzzle known as a "necktie." Put a word in the blank space so that, when the word has been read twice as you go around the tie, it will make the sentence complete and correct.

A RAILROAD PUZZLE

Fill the blank spaces with the name of something (plural) that is very important in railroading so that the other letters will make a word, reading horizontally and vertically.

A BOOK CHARADE

This is a very clever charade.

My first is in page, but never in book.
My second in cut, is never in cook.
My third is in zebra, and never in cat.
My fourth is in zebu, but never in rat.
My fifth is in vessel, and isn't in row
My sixth is in see, but never in show.
Each page that you turn you will hurry and look.
It's the name of a favorite game in this book.

UP-SIDE-DOWN-SIDE-UP

SEE THE WINDMILL ON THE HILL
WITH THE ARMS THAT FLAP AND FLY
TURN THE PICTURE AND YOU'LL SEE
TRILISA'S NICE NEW TIE - - -

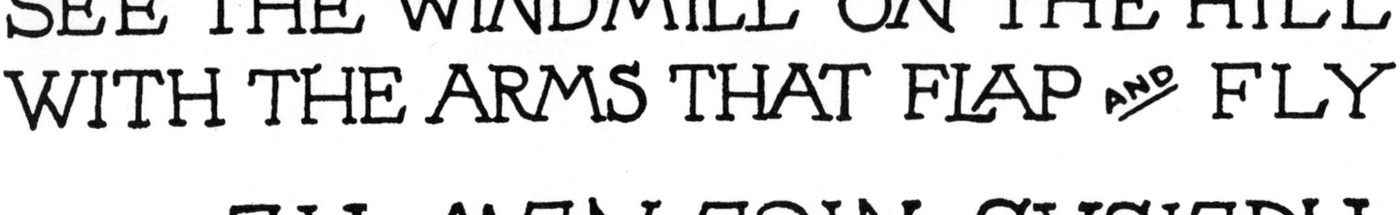

A RIDDLE

If a room with *eight* corners—heigho,
Had a cat in each corner, you know,
And *seven* black cats before every cat,
And a cat *on each tail*—think of that!
This is a cat[ch] riddle, you see,
How many in all would there be?

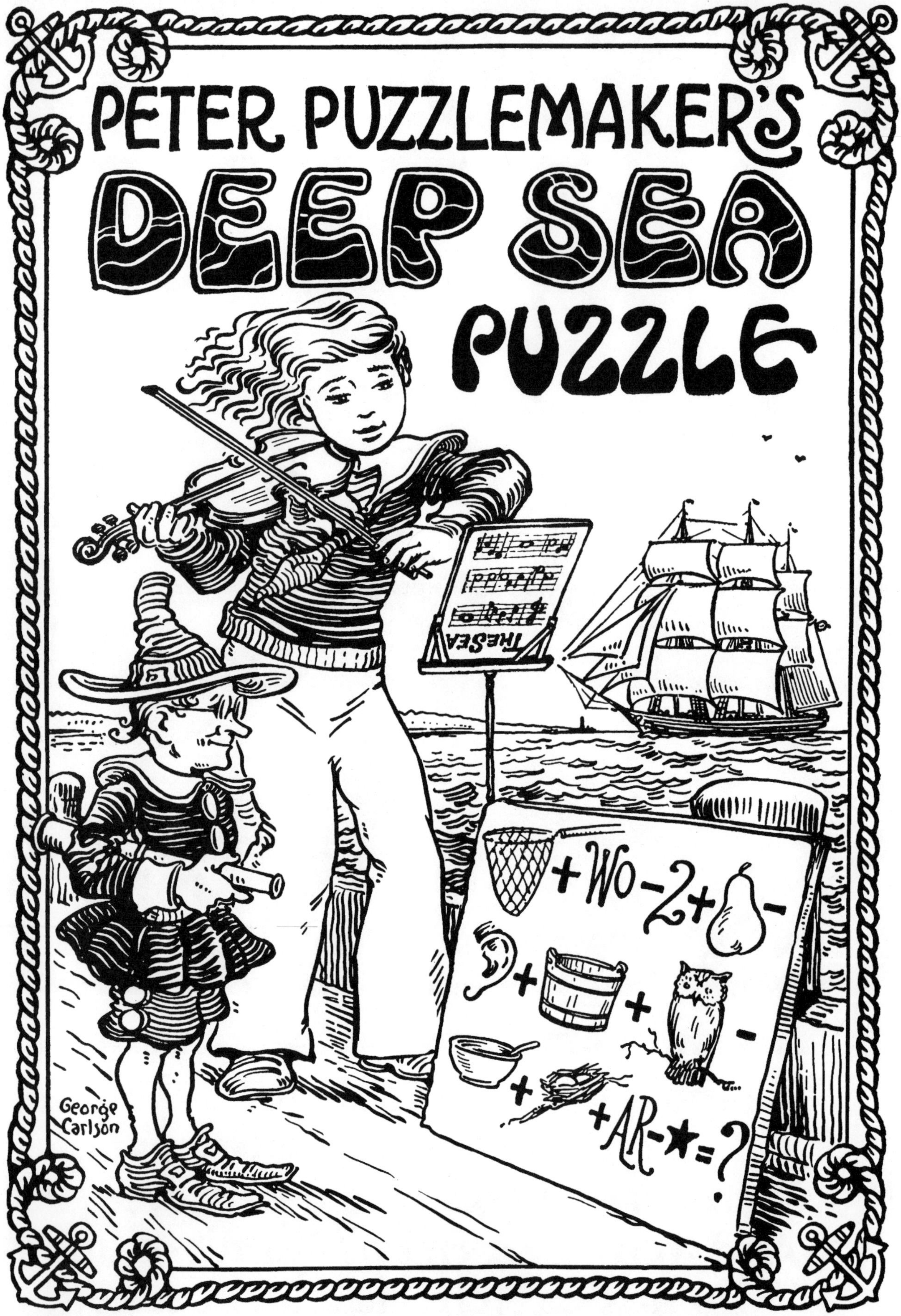

THERE is a tang of the salt sea air and the fresh breeze from the ocean as we go to solve this puzzle. Add and subtract the pictures on the sign and you will get not only the name of the ship that you see out there in the harbor, but also of a being supposed to live in the sea. The sailor is playing us some lively nautical music, but something is wrong in the picture.

A SALT SEA WORD DIAMOND

Here is a word diamond. Fill in the blank spaces with the name of something found on all ships so that the other letters will make words reading both horizontally and vertically.

HIDDEN BIRDS IN DEEP SEA WORDS

Hidden in these sentences are the names of six familiar birds.

We were halfway over the Pacific on Doris's birthday.

How unusual to be in the Atlantic rowing in a frail boat.

The fast clipper ship had overtaken us by this time.

The port and starboard lights, those well-known signals of the sea, gleamed brightly in the night.

The admiral boarded one ship as the other one stood by.

There she saw the flag on the top spar rotating in the wind.

A SEASHORE PUZZLE

The words in this picture, which is in anagram, represent something we will always find at the seashore. Just put the letters into their proper order and you will know what it is.

A SHIP REBUS

This rebus, or picture puzzle, represents the name of a part of a ship. Any puzzler who has read sea stories will easily solve this.

WORD JUMPING

By changing one letter in the word at a time, make FOUR into FIVE in eight moves.

F O U R

— — — —

— — — —

— — — —

— — — —

— — — —

— — — —

— — — —

F I V E

UP-SIDE-DOWN-SIDE-UP

OH SEE FUNNY LITTLE ELVES!
WHAT MAKES THEM HURRY SO?
JUST TURN THE PICTURE UPSIDE DOWN
AND THEN YOU'LL SURELY KNOW!

MY first is in sweet but not in sour;
My second's in minute but not in hour;
My third is in ice cream but not in cake;
My fourth is in river and also in lake.
My whole is something that ever flies,
Yet has no wings. Guess, if you're wise.

The other day the pie maker made up the names of my four favorite pies in a puzzle. There are two sets of pictures to the puzzle. Take the five in each set and write their names down in four letters each. When arranged in proper order, the first and third letters in each set will spell the names of my favorite pies. Then rearrange the letters in the sign on the counter and another type of pie will be "plain" as day. Also find what is wrong in the shop.

WORD JUMPING

By changing one letter in the word at a time, make BUY PIE in five moves.

B U Y

— — —

— — —

— — —

— — —

P I E

FLOWER WORD SQUARE

Fill the blank spaces with the name of a flower so that the other letters will make true words, reading both horizontally and vertically.

AN ANIMAL CHARADE

My first in wood is not in tree.
My next in trap is not in free.
My third in cold is not in heat.
My fourth in paws is not in feet.
My fifth in smell is not in trail.
My sixth in quick and also quail.
My next in stem is not in bend.
My whole a furry woodland friend.

PUZZLE PIE

Speaking of pie, here is another pie puzzle. These words look pretty jumbled up, but after you have arranged the letters properly, they will make a well-known rhyme.

Lispem Minos emt a napiem,
Nogig ot het rafi;
Yass Meplis Osnim ot eht menaip,
"Tel em state royu erwa."

Sysa eth apnemi ot Pelsim Noism,
"Wosh em strif oryu nepyn."
Asys Emspil Niosm ot het nimape,
"Dieden, I vahe ton yan."

A SCHOOL PUZZLE

The teacher is calling on one of her students to recite. By changing the letters in the picture into their proper order, you can make the name of the lesson Peg is now studying.

ONE moonlit night I met an old witch. As we were talking, ten big bats suddenly flew across the sky, and as they passed in front of the moon I thought of a very good puzzle. Four straight lines properly placed across the moon would put each bat in a space by itself. The witch also showed me a puzzle sum. By adding and subtracting, you will make a word important to witches. And can you find the mistake in the picture?

PETER PUZZLEMAKER'S CHAT

WORD JUMPING

By changing one letter in the word at a time, make SHOE into COAT in five moves.

S H O E

— — — —

— — — —

— — — —

— — — —

C O A T

PRECIOUS STONE WORD SQUARE

Fill the blank spaces with the name of a precious stone so that the other letters will make true words, reading both horizontally and vertically.

ANOTHER WITCH PUZZLE

The witch is looking for something that is very necessary for her games. Her cat is telling you what it is, but you will have to put the letters into their proper order to find the answer.

A SUMMER PUZZLE

This "moving" picture certainly does not suggest summer, but if you take the letters in the funny title and change them around into their proper order it will spell something that we all have been looking for.

This is a portrait of Mister McGee
His cheerful expression is pleasant to see.

While here is the gloomy Cornelius McZall
I'm sure I don't care for his picture at all.

A LITTLE round house is under a tree;
It hides from you, it hides from me;
But if we can find it, we'll have a treat;
For little round house is full of good meat.

What is it?

WHILE I am carving, you can change one letter in the word at a time to go from NECK to WING in five moves. But the main course in this puzzle dinner is a picture acrostic. Each of the small pictures represents a four-letter word, and these, when placed in the spaces on the turkey's tail feathers, should read in toward the center. One letter will do for the ending of all the words. The first letters will spell a word meaning "parts of a fowl." A mistake is waiting to be found by sharp eyes.

WORD JUMPING

By changing one letter in the word at a time, make FIRE into COOK in four moves.

F I R E

_ _ _ _

_ _ _ _

_ _ _ _

C O O K

A TIMELY WISH

Jesse is looking eagerly at the calendar, and I am sure you can guess what he is wishing for. If you can't, just rearrange the letters in the upper part of the calendar and you will have the answer.

AT THE ZOO

Here we see Willie visiting the birdhouse at the zoo. He is looking at a bird that interests him. Fill in the blank spaces in the diamond with the name of this bird so that it reads both down and across. Then the other letters will also make true words.

A STORE PUZZLE

Jane has forgotten what she went to the store for, but we can help her by solving this puzzle. Fill the blank spaces in the diamond with the correct words so that it reads both down and across. Then the other letters will also make true words.

And here is a picture of Major O'Hearn
His mustache is long and expression is stern.
George Carlson
Jonathan Jenkins is meager and slim
His hat has a wide and a worn-out brim.

A BIG red ball fell from a tree;
It said, "Why yes, you can eat me."
A small boy ate it and he cried,
"Oh, see the brown babies asleep inside!"

What was the ball?

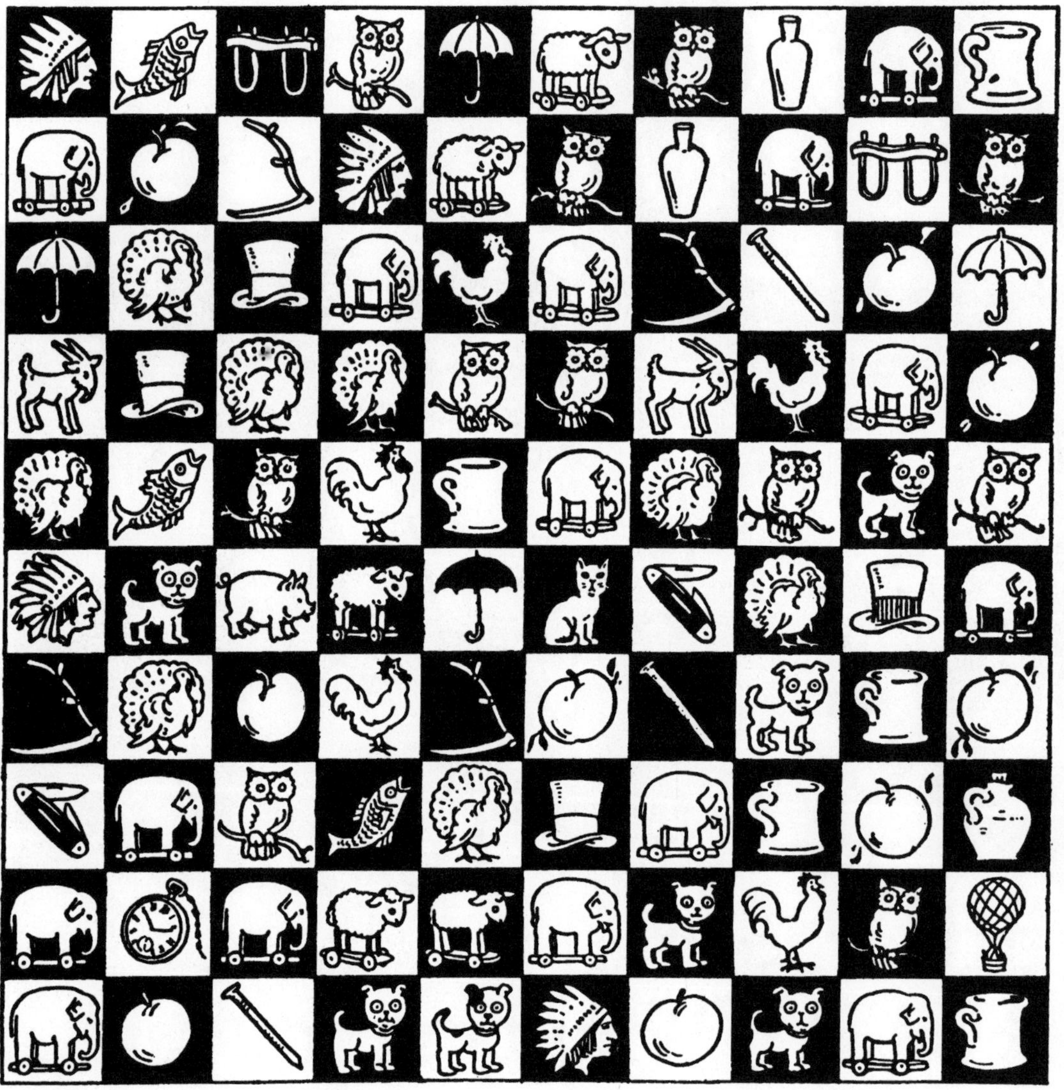

Write down the first letter of each object's name. Read the letters from left to right, top to bottom, and you'll uncover a secret Valentine's Day message!

Note: The third picture on the opposite page is a *yoke,* once used on American farms for hitching oxen together. And the pictures above that look like rulers should be called *yardsticks.*

ANSWERS

ANSWERS

Some pages are not listed here because they do not require answers.

PAGE 2 Peter Puzzlemaker's Happy New Year Puzzle

Old, odd, add, aid, lid, lad, law, paw, pew, new.

Motto: *It's never too late to mend.*

Mistake: On the clock dial, 3, 6, and 9 are written backward.

PAGE 3 Peter Puzzlemaker's Puzzle About Washington

The words in Washington are: wash, ash, inn, goat, win, shin, ton, saw, song, wish.

Motto: *In union there is strength.*

Mistake: The sign is not resting on the post, so there is not much "union," is there?

PAGE 4 Peter Puzzlemaker's Valentine

Peter says the words in Valentine are: tan, tin, tea, even, vane, tale, nine, vine, lane, neat, alive, vat, ten, net, lean, lent.

Motto: *Look before you leap.*

Missing: The buckle on one of Peter's shoes.

PAGE 5 Peter Puzzlemaker and the Puzzle Menu

Peter's lunch menu is: chicken, rice, pickles, eggplant, pie, ice cream.

Motto: *Half a loaf is better than none.*

Mistake: The water in the carafe is not level.

PAGE 7 UP~DOWN

An umbrella.

PAGE 8 Peter Puzzlemaker and the Hidden Boys' Names

The hidden names are: James, William, Walter, Kyle, Howard, Ernest, Earle, Fred, José, Arthur.

Mistake: Two of the birds are flying upside down.

PAGE 9 Peter Puzzlemaker and the 3 Matches

Leaving the first match as it was, Peter

arranged the other two into a V, making IV.

To take one from three and leave ten, Lynette Elf first had III. With

the second and third I's she made X, which gave her IX. Taking I away left him X, which is Roman for ten.

Motto: *The more haste the less speed.*

Note: Something was said to be missing from the picture, but nothing about this is mentioned in the picture's answers. I have searched in vain for a mistake. It can't be a missing leg of the stool because the leg could be hidden behind Peter's right leg. It can't be missing black color on Peter's jacket below the lowest button because the white spot there is part of Peter's white belt.

In the far distance there seems to be something absent from the top of the church's steeple, if it is a steeple, but this almost invisible detail is not typical of Carlson's usually obvious errors. It seems unlikely that Carlson would have forgotten to omit something. My wife came up with the cleverest suggestion: The missing thing in the picture is a mistake! — M. G.

PAGE 10 Peter Puzzlemaker's 3 Sentences

The missing words in the three sentences are as follows: Vote, veto. Stop, pots, spot. Shoe, hose, hoes.

Mistake: The back cover of the book is wider than the front.

PAGE 11 Peter Puzzlemaker and the Hidden Girls' Names

The hidden names are: Nell, Kit, Nan, Leslie, Sara, Joy, Melissa, Angela, Linda, Sandy.

The name of the country is Chili.

Mistake: The nose piece of Peter's glasses is missing.

PAGE 13 Kit~T

When you're teasin' it.

PAGE 14 Peter Puzzlemaker's Tangled Presidents Puzzle

Peter is curious to know how many of you solved the Presidents Puzzle. "That was a hard one," says he, but I believe you have fooled him. This diagram shows how your line should go. The Presidents' names are, in order, Harding, Washington, Taft, Lincoln, Grant, Jefferson, Roosevelt, McKinley, Polk, Monroe.

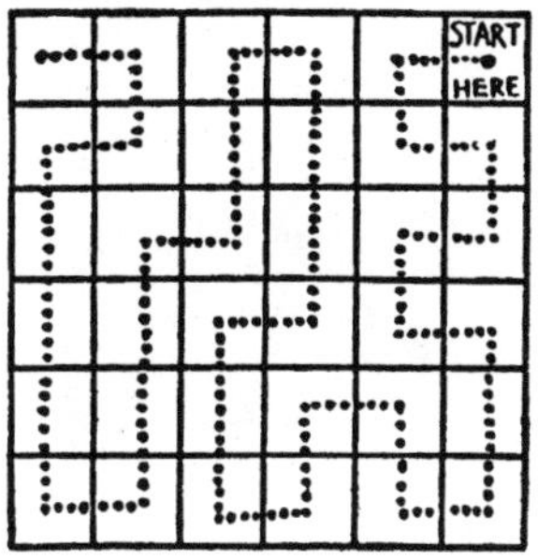

The sign reads, *No gains without pains.*

Mistake: Peter's shoe buckles do not match.

PAGE 15 Peter Puzzlemaker and the Lost Words

The lost words are tea, eat, ate. Meat, tame, mate. Amy, may, yam.

Motto: *A stitch in time saves nine.*

Mistake: The hammer has three prongs.

PAGE 16 Peter Puzzlemaker and the Broken Checkerboard

Here is a diagram of the solution. The upper picture shows the board in the same position that it is in Peter's hand. The piece that is cut out fits exactly by turning it once to the right. It makes a perfect square with eight checkers on a side.

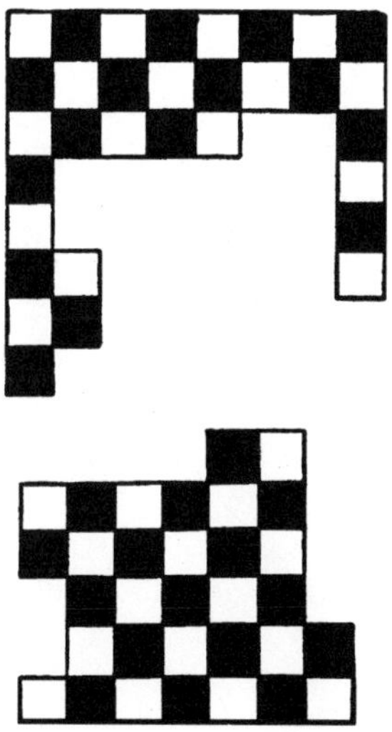

Country: The monogram spells *China (CH-in-A).*

Mistake: Peter's left shoe has no heel and the tongue of that shoe is much shorter than that of the right.

PAGE 17 Peter Puzzlemaker and the Balloons

The names that Peter was able to find were James, Lester, Charles, Sam, Henry, Carl, Chester, Mac, Earl, Al, and Ernest. Perhaps you found others.

Mistake: The balloon seller's left thumb is on the wrong side of her hand.

The sign should read, "In the air."

PAGE 18 3 Puzzle Notes

The answers to the puzzle notes, or *doublets,* as they are called, are: Dear, dare, read. Plate, pleat, petal. Forest, foster, softer.

PAGE 19 Where Are They?

One of the cows is upside down in the tree on the right, and the other is upside down under the fence. One of the horses is about the shoer's neck, and the other is about the sign.

PAGE 22 Peter Puzzlemaker and His Pond

The solution of the pond puzzle is found in the diagram.

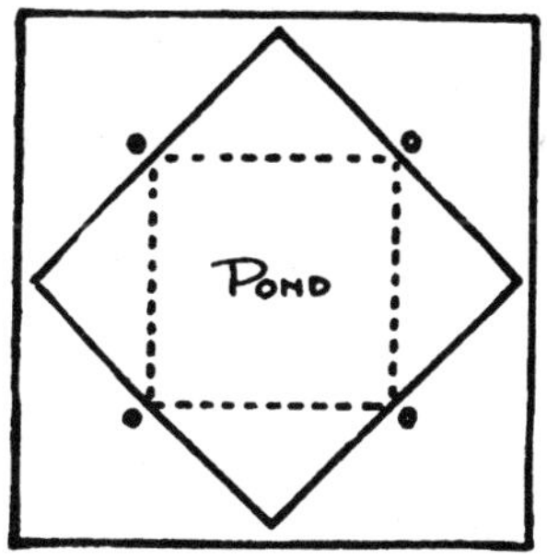

The sign reads, "You must not fish in this pond."

Mistake: The reflections of the trees in the pond are in different directions.

PAGE 23 Peter Puzzlemaker's Mixed Flowers

The diagram shows how to find the flower names. They are: carnation, tulip, pansy, rose, dahlia, hollyhock, and larkspur. The name on the box is *Aster*.

Mistake: I'll wager I had you hunting for what was missing. There are no holes in the flower pots. Your plants wouldn't flourish long in pots as I drew them, would they?

PAGE 24 Peter Puzzlemaker's Puzzle Signs

1. Alter, alert, later. 2. Dear, dare, read. 3. Star, rats, arts.

The sign reads, "Believe in yourself."

Mistake: The third sign carrier is not holding the sign.

PAGE 25 Peter Puzzlemaker's Can Puzzle

Peter has a long answer this time, for there were fifteen cans to name. Here they are:

1. Canal
2. Canopy
3. Cane
4. Candy
5. Candle
6. Canary
7. Canister
8. Cannon
9. Canteen
10. Canvas
11. Canoe
12. Cantilever
13. Cantaloupe
14. Canyon
15. Canada

Ami is going to spend two dollars (doll-R's).

Mistake: One of Peter's eyeglass lenses is plain and the other is rimmed.

PAGE 26 Peter Puzzlemaker's "A" Puzzle

abode
academy
accordion
acorn
advertisement
aerial
aim
airplane
airship
alley
ambulance
anchor
animal
ankles
annex
announcement
anvil
apartments
apostrophe
applause
apple
apron
aquarium
arc lamp
arch
archer
archway
ark
arm
armchair
arrow
artist
atlas
attic
audience
auto
aviator
awning
ax

PAGE 27 Peter Puzzlemaker's "B" Puzzle

baby
back
background
bacon
badge
bag
baggage
baker
bakery
balcony
bale
ball
balloon
balustrade
bananas
band
banister
bank
banner
bar
barber
barbershop
bark
barrel
baseball
basket
bat
bay
bay window
beach
beacon
beak
beard
beast
bed
bedroom
beef
beets
belfry
bell
belt
beverage
bib
bicycle
bill
biped
bird
blade
blinders
blinds
blonde
blouse
board
boat
body
bonnet
book
bottle
bough
bouquet

bow
bowl
bowsprit
box
boy
bracelet
bracket
branch
bread
breakwater
breast
brick
bridge
bridle
brig
brim
brook
broom
brow
bucket
buckle
buggy
building
bundle
buns
buoy
bureau
bush
bushel
butcher
butterfly
button

PAGE 30 Peter Puzzlemaker's Christmas Tree

The presents in the packages were: boat, ball, bat, doll, roller skates, ark, drum, marbles, book, and skis.

Tito Elf's card should read, "Holiday Greeting."

Mistake: The word *friend* is spelled incorrectly.

PAGE 31 Peter Puzzlemaker's Winter Puzzle

Peter says everybody must have guessed this puzzle, it was so easy. If you found the right letters, they spelled *Jack Frost*.

The sign may be either *Spain*, *snail,* or *stair*.

Mistake: One of the crow's feet has sprouted four toes instead of three.

PAGE 32 Peter Puzzlemaker and the Puzzle Package

The package Peter received contained a valentine, for the words are: Vane, Alps, Lips, Ears, Nose, Toes, Inch, Note, East.

Mistake: Peter's spectacles have but one side.

The letters on the flowerpot, rearranged, spell *geranium*.

PAGE 33 Peter Puzzlemaker's Gem Puzzle

The precious stones are: di-amo-nd, pe-arl, em-era-ld, sap-ph-i-re, r-ub-y, mo-on-st-one.

Ana's sign says *platinum*.

Mistake: The flags atop the buildings are waving in different directions.

PAGE 35 A Timely Riddle

A watch.

PAGE 36 Peter Puzzlemaker in Springtime

HAND – AND + YACHT + HORN – THORN + AND – HAND + INCH + URN – CHURN – THREE + L – REEL = HYACINTH.

Mistake: The windows are missing on the houses.

PAGE 37 Peter Puzzlemaker's Concealed Presidents

The hidden names of Presidents are: 1. Garfield. 2. Taft. 3. Harding. 4. Washington. 5. Harrison.

Joshua Crow's sign should read *Carter*.

Mistake: Joshua has an extra toe on each foot.

PAGE 38 Peter Puzzlemaker's Fruit Puzzle

The state is California.

Hilary Elf's puzzle says *Grapes*.

Mistake: The grass is blown on one side of the tree and not on the other.

PAGE 39 Peter Puzzlemaker's Seven Animals

The hidden animals are: otter, monkey, beaver, horse, sheep, badger, buffalo.

Edgar Elf's rebus puzzle says *Donkey (D-on-key)*.

Mistake: The giraffe's horns are missing.

PAGE 42 Peter Puzzlemaker and the Two Animals

Rabbit and donkey:

ROAD
AL**S**O
BEAN
BOO**K**
I**D**LE
TRA**Y**

The dog's name is Prince.

Mistake: The white cuff is missing from Peter's right sleeve.

PAGE 43 Peter Puzzlemaker's Hidden Animals

The hidden animals are: lion, camel, tiger, panther, calf, cow, weasel.

The puzzle advice is: *If the grate be empty, put coal on.* You may not get that even after you see the answer written out. Just study that puzzle until you see it.

Mistake: Peter's cane is not finished.

PAGE 44 Peter Puzzlemaker's Hidden Presidents

1. Adams. 2. Jackson. 3. Lincoln. 4. Johnson. 5. Hayes.

The book title is *History*.

Mistake: The books on the shelves are upside down.

PAGE 45 Peter Puzzlemaker's Dinner Puzzle

Peter's Thanksgiving dinner fairly makes my mouth water just to write about it. He had:

soup	turkey
celery	bread
butter	potatoes
beans	cranberries
pie	ice cream
coffee	tea

Peter's guest was saying, as you would expect her to, *"Thank you."*

Mistake: Did you discover that the *wings of the turkey were missing?* If you especially like wings, you saw that at once.

PAGE 47 A Riddle

Lumps of sugar.

PAGE 48 Peter Puzzlemaker's Review

Address Puzzle: The address on the letter should read, *A. Underwood, Andover, Mass.* Easy, isn't it? A under wood and over mass! Ha!

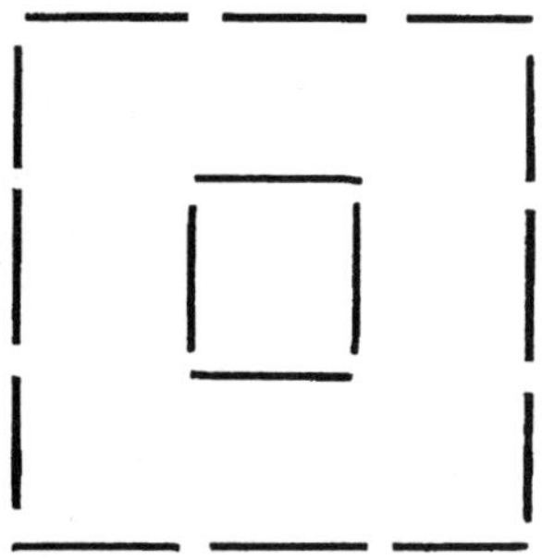

Toothpick Puzzle: Were you able to take eight toothpicks away and leave two squares? This is the way to do it:

A Puzzle Note:
Doctor Long expects Dr. Short to explain the misunderstanding between them.

PAGE 49 Peter Puzzlemaker's Review

Puzzle Sum: MONKEY – KEY + INFANT – ON – FAN + NOTE – TT + W – E = MINNOW.

The One-Person Game has such a variety of moves that it is really more of a game than a puzzle, but Peter has published it anyway and is sure that you will have fun playing it.

The Multiplication Sign Puzzle: The diagram here shows how the pieces should be put together.

A Mixed-up Recitation:

Mary had a little lamb,
Its fleece was white as snow.
And everywhere that Mary went,
The lamb was sure to go!

PAGE 50 Hidden Geography

The answers are: 1. Fla. 2. Md. 3. Ga. 4. La. 5. Tex. 6. Miss. 7. Ky. 8. Tenn. 9. Mo. 10. Wis.

PAGE 51 Who Is the Biggest?
The bunny is the tallest.

PAGE 53 What Am I?
An onion.

PAGE 54 Peter Puzzlemaker's Radio Puzzle
Pittsburgh, Los Angeles. (**P**ai**l**, **i**nt**o**, **t**op**s**, **t**og**a**, **s**ig**n**, **b**u**g**, **u**k**e**, **r**ol**l**, **g**at**e**, **h**oe**s**.)
Mistake: The loudspeaker is not connected.

PAGE 55 Peter Puzzlemaker's Chat
A Rebus: President Tyler.
Word Jumping: Blue, blur, slur, spur, spar, spat, seat, sent, pent, pint, pink.
A Rainy Day Puzzle: April Shower.
Riddle Corner: 1. Go around with the world. 2. Because seven ate nine. 3. What goes in it. 4. When it gets to the bottom. 5. Gets wet.

PAGE 56 Peter Puzzlemaker's Cat and Dog Puzzle
Black cat, clack hat, crack hot, track hoe, trace toe, trice foe, trite fox, write fog, white dog.
Missing: One side of eyebrows and whiskers on the cat.

PAGE 57 Peter Puzzlemaker's Chat
Is It a Valentine? Wise owl and the moon.
A Flower Charade: Sunflower.
Word Jumping: Owl, oil, ail, aid, bid, bad, bat.
A Rebus: Argentina (R-gent-in-A).
A Kitchen Charade: Salt.

PAGE 59
A potato.

PAGE 60 Peter Puzzlemaker's Star Puzzle
Venus. (1–Voice. 2–Erase. 3–Noise. 4–Unite. 5–Skate.)
Orion. (1–Olive. 2–Rinse. 3–Image. 4–Ozone. 5–Niece.)
Mistake: The roof line does not show behind the open window.

PAGE 61 Peter Puzzlemaker's Chat
Presidential Word Square: Lincoln.
Double Acrostic: Whittier, Tennyson. 1. Want. 2. Home. 3. Iron. 4. Town. 5. Tray. 6. Iris. 7. Echo. 8. Rain.
Hidden Countries: India, New Zealand, Canada, Peru, Kenya, Sweden.
A Musical Charade: Violin.
The Riddle Corner: 1. Kittens. 2. A skating pond. 3. When it has blinds on.

PAGE 62 Peter Puzzlemaker's Park Puzzle
The paths would be as in this diagram.
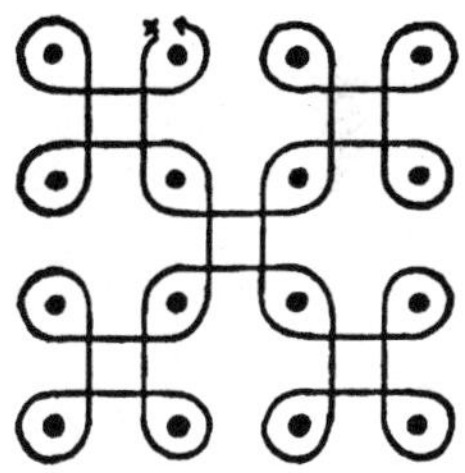
Mistake: The shadows of the trees on the extreme left are missing.

PAGE 63 Peter Puzzlemaker's Chat
Girl's Name Word Square: Dorothy.
A Rebus: Denmark.
Word Jumping: Door, doom, loom, look, lock.
A Puzzle Sum: PO + LEMON – POLE + KEY = MONKEY.
Hidden Cities: 1. Paris. 2. Berlin. 3. Athens. 4. Madrid. 5. London.

PAGE 64 Peter Puzzlemaker's "C" Puzzle
cage
calendar
calf
canary
candy
cans
cap
card
carrots
carton
case
cash register
cat
ceiling
celery
chain
chair
cheeks
cheese
chest
chevron
child

chimney
chin
church
circle
clerk
clothes
cloud
cobweb
coffee
coin
collar
cone
cord
core
cork
corkscrew
corner
cottage
counter
couple
cover
cracks
crackers
crate
creases
cross
crown
cuff
cupboard
curb
curls
curtain
customer
cut
cutlery
cylinder

PAGE 65 Peter Puzzlemaker's "D" Puzzle

daisies
date
daughter
daylight
decanter
decoration
deer
degree
delivery person
dentist
design
desk
dessert
detour
diamond
dictionary
digger
dimples
dinner
dinosaur
diploma
dishes
disk
distance
ditch
doctor
documents
dog
doily
doll
dollar
dome
dominoes
donkey
door
doorknob
doorway
dormer window
doughnuts
draperies
drawer
drawing
dress
drink
driver
dwelling

PAGE 66 Mix-Ups

Birds fly, ice melts, fish swim, acorns grow, cats scratch, crayons color, paper tears, flowers bloom, iron rusts, pigs grunt, windows open, knives cut, frogs croak, babies play, children learn, cows moo, fire burns, rabbits hop, parents work, owls hoot.

If you matched babies with learn, and children with play, you may count both as correct also.

PAGE 68 Peter Puzzlemaker's Travel Puzzle

N.Y., N.J., Vt., Del., La., Va., Pa.

City: Washington.

Mistake: The train is coming on the wrong track.

PAGE 69 Peter Puzzlemaker's Chat

Hidden Flowers: 1. Aster; 2. Daisy; 3. Geranium; 4. Rose; 5. Pansy.

A Necktie Puzzle: Noticed (Not iced).

A Railroad Puzzle: Signals.

A Book Charade: Puzzle.

PAGE 71 A Riddle

Eight cats.

PAGE 72 Peter Puzzlemaker's Deep Sea Puzzle

NET + WO – TWO + PEAR – EAR + TUB + OWL – BOWL + NEST + AR – STAR = NEPTUNE.

Mistake: The sailor's sheet music is upside down.

PAGE 73 Peter Puzzlemaker's Chat

A Salt Sea Word Diamond: Sailors.

Hidden Birds: Condor, crow, dove, eagle, heron, parrot.

A Seashore Puzzle: Ocean breezes.

A Ship Rebus: Forcastle.

Word Jumping: Four, foul, fool, foot, fort, form, firm, fire, five.

PAGE 75

Time.

PAGE 76 Peter Puzzlemaker in the Pie Shop

1. Arms. 2. Pail. 3. Pens. 4. Lace. 5. Eyes (Apple–Mince).

1. Pole. 2. Eyes. 3. Arms. 4. Crow. 5. Hand (Peach–Lemon).

Anagram: Pineapple.

Mistake: The i's on the sign should not be dotted.

PAGE 77 Peter Puzzlemaker's Chat

Word Jumping: Buy, boy, toy, toe, tie, pie.

Flower Word Square: Fuchsia.

An Animal Charade: Opossum.

Puzzle Pie: The rhyme is the well-known "Simple Simon met a pieman."

A School Puzzle: Geography.

PAGE 78 Peter Puzzlemaker's Moon Puzzle

The diagram here shows how to separate the bats with four lines.

Puzzle sum: MAGNET – NET + ICE – E = MAGIC.

Mistake: Peter's shadow faces backward.

PAGE 79 Peter Puzzlemaker's Chat

Word Jumping: Shoe, shop, chop, chap, chat, coat.

Another Witch Puzzle: Broomstick.

Precious Stone Word Square: Diamond.

A Summer Puzzle: Vacation time.

PAGE 81

A nut.

PAGE 82 Peter Puzzlemaker's Turkey Puzzle

Neck, nick, nice, nine, wine, wing.

Acrostic: Giblets. 1. Gems. 2. Inks. 3. Boys. 4. Lips. 5. Ears. 6. Tops. 7. Sums.

Mistake: Peter is carving with the back of his knife.

PAGE 83 Peter Puzzlemaker's Chat

Word Jumping: Fire, fore, fork, cork, cook.

A Timely Wish: Holidays.

At the Zoo: Pelican.

A Store Puzzle: Mustard.

PAGE 85

An apple.

PAGES 86, 87 The Valentine

If you love me as I love you,
There's naught too great for me to do.
I'd pluck the stars and make of them
A jewelled robe and diadem.

I'd build a palace and a throne
Of gold I made from common stone.
Then I would pay you homage true,
And give it all and more to you.

—John Martin

To this sentimental message I can only add, "Do, re, ___, 2." —M. G.